Corporate Fund Raising
A Practical Plan of Action
by W. Grant Brownrigg

CORPORATE FUND RAISING:

A PRACTICAL PLAN OF ACTION

BY

W. GRANT BROWNRIGG

EXECUTIVE DIRECTOR

GREATER HARTFORD ARTS COUNCIL

AMERICAN COUNCIL FOR THE ARTS

For additional copies please send $12.50 to ACA, 570 Seventh Avenue
New York, NY 10018. Price includes postage and handling.

American Council for the Arts (ACA) gratefully acknowledges
the generous grant of the Shell Companies Foundation
for the publication of this book.

i

CONTENTS

PREFACE

This booklet describes in detail a practical and systematic approach to soliciting contributions from business firms. Its focus is on arts councils and it is based on the experience of the Greater Hartford Arts Council in Hartford, Connecticut. Although Hartford may be unique because of the high degree of corporate involvement in community affairs, the precepts and methodology outlined here can be applied to any location and any type of nonprofit fund raising.

INTRODUCTION

Soliciting corporations for contributions is a selling process. Like any marketing effort, it must be directed at the potential customer — with the customer's needs, likes, and dislikes in mind. Customers must be convinced that the "product" presented to them is worthy of their support and will produce benefits that outweigh investments. Thus, the basic steps in developing a corporate fund raising strategy are to identify the market and its needs, to package a "product" that will address those needs, and to develop an approach that is both effective and efficient.

The major activities in a corporate fund raising program may be divided into seven phases:

1. Market Identification
2. Product Development and Packaging
3. Campaign Strategy
4. Organization
5. Precampaign Activities
6. The Campaign
7. Postcampaign Activities

In general, these activities should be undertaken in the sequence outlined below. However, in particular circumstances changes may be required.

Scheduling

Before any major activities are undertaken, the first step in implementing a fund raising campaign is to draw up a schedule showing the target dates for the completion of major activities. Once the dates for the campaign are set, the timing of preparations can be determined by working backwards from the dates when they need to be completed. For example, if the kick-off is scheduled for January 15 and the materials to be handed out at that time require two months to complete, then the development of materials must begin November 15. The schedule should be translated into a week-by-week activity sheet showing specific tasks, hours required for completion, and delegation of responsibilities. Exhibit A includes a sample schedule drawn up along these lines.

MARKET IDENTIFICATION

At the outset, a broad definition of the market should be made, establishing the geographic area and the types and sizes of companies to be approached during the campaign. A broad geographic area would encompass more firms and would yield potentially more dollars — but campaigning in such an area also requires more solicitors, more coordination, and extended services. So a balance must be sought. One guideline often used is to include the core city plus those surrounding areas normally included with the city by the Chamber of Commerce, the United Way, a regional government, or educational bodies. If there is no such "definition" of an area, establish an area that best suits your agency, weighing the factors of cost, possible returns, and required services. (Keep in mind, too, that out-of-pocket expenses can mount up. For a full-scale campaign to solicit 1,000 companies, these expenses should not exceed $5,000. Cost estimates based on the Greater Hartford Arts Council's 1977 campaign are shown in Exhibit B.)

Once the geographic area has been selected, the next question is whether all companies, regardless of size or industry, are to be considered potential prospects. If firms of all sizes are potential prospects, the magnitude of the campaign can be enormous. However, major donors often feel that a large number of contributors is important because it indicates broad community support for the endeavor. Furthermore, the more firms approached, the more people become aware of the importance of the arts. For these reasons, the campaign should encompass businesses of any size and all industries, trades, and professions, including law, accounting, medicine, and dentistry. A firm should not be excluded from the campaign on a categorical basis but only as a result of practical constraints, such as time and personnel, or special circumstance in a particular area.

The Prospect List

The next step is to draw up a list of companies to be approached, recognizing that the longer the list, the more solicitors will be required, the more work there will be for mailings, record-keeping, and other routine activities. The most serious danger in preparing the list is a failure to take into account practical limitations of time, personnel, and other resources required for the campaign.

Between 1976 and 1977, the Greater Hartford Arts Council increased its prospect list from 220 to 960 firms and its number of fund-drive workers from 35 to more than 200. This vast expansion required a massive amount of time and effort: recruiting solicitors took more than two months of full-time telephoning; verifying information took more than four workweeks.

The best way to avoid the danger of excessive expansion is to set a time limit for the preparation of the list and a numerical limit on the prospects. The list should be completed within two months, and at least six months prior to the campaign kick-off. The target number of prospects to be established depends not only on the size of the current list but also on the projected number of solicitors. As will be discussed later, each solicitor should be assigned no more than five prospects; thus, a minimum of 200 solicitors must be recruited for 1,000 prospects.

The prospect list itself can be developed from many sources of information. Among the most useful are:

- current prospects and contributors, the core of the list
- lists developed for other fund drives, such as the United Way
- Dun & Bradstreet, which has data for most sizable firms in most areas
- business directories published by Chambers of Commerce or economic development agencies
- Departments of Labor and Commerce (particularly for new industry)
- Yellow Pages in the telephone book
- personal contact: businesses spotted while driving; business people met at parties, etc.
- evaluation committee (see below)

If the list contains more than 100 names, there may be advantages in computerization. Data-processing concerns such as the Burroughs Corporation are often willing to donate program and computer assistance. Computerization permits accurate and frequent updating of information and makes it possible to sort and print the prospect list in a variety of ways: by industry (SIC code), contribution level, geographic area, and solicitor. Furthermore, the computer can print items requiring individual company names such as labels, pledge cards, and invoices.

Exhibit C is a sample format for a computerized list.

Information about each firm should be limited to that which is clearly useful. Excessive data—facts that are "nice to know" but not essential—will only complicate and overburden the system. The basic information is the name, address, and telephone number of the company as well as the name of the person to be contacted (the president, if there is no other specified contact). Two or three years of the company's contributions history, including names of previous solicitors, is also essential.

Certain other data are useful though not absolutely essential. The Standard Industrial Classification (SIC) code number indicates the type of business in which a particular company is engaged. It is obtainable for each industry from the federal government's Standard Industrial Classification Manual. Measures of business volume, such as total sales and number of employees, are also important. These figures, together with the SIC code, can be used in making comparisons among firms.

After the prospect list has been compiled, the name, address, telephone number, and contact's name must be verified by telephone. Misspelled names or wrong phone numbers frustrate and annoy both prospect and solicitor and will hamper the entire fund raising effort. The verification process should begin three months before the kick-off. On an average, 90 such telephone calls can be made in an eight-hour day.

Although the core list must be readied six months before the beginning of the campaign, important prospects may be added to the list as late as the final month before the kick-off. The number of changes allowed depends on the progress of the rest of the campaign preparations, the potential gift size, and the feasibility of recruiting additional solicitors to handle new prospects.

Prospect Evaluation

One of the most critical aspects of the entire campaign is determining how much money to ask each company to contribute. Too low a determination will result in getting less money than possible; too high a determination will lead to unrealistic expectations for the total goal. An excessively high request may also so affront a prospect that the company will give little or nothing. In essence, the request must be as realistic as possible, though slightly higher than the actual amount expected.

A practical and tested mechanism for determining the amount of each request is the evaluation committee. This group should be made up of approximately 15 members and should include previous solicitors, business executives (especially bankers), and individuals from a variety of fields with an in-depth knowledge of the community and local businesses. As soon as the prospect list has been drawn up this committee should meet to review every name on the list and determine the amount to be asked of each.

There are six general methods for determining how much a company should give. No single method seems to be applicable in every case; a combination of some of these measures probably provides the most beneficial results.

1. *Previous contribution.* Add a certain percentage (for example, 10 percent) to a donor's previous gift.

   The two major defects of this approach are that it is applicable only to current or past givers, not to new prospects, and it tends to restrict the increase to a maximum of 10 percent.

7

2. *Comparison*. Compare the giving level of a particular company with that of a similar firm.

   Properly applied, "peer pressure" can work extremely well to bring low-givers up to the average. However, it can also work in reverse and cause a giver to reduce a donation. If there are no bases for comparison within a given area, other arts councils or ACA (American Council for the Arts) may be able to supply information on comparable firms in other areas.

3. *Number of employees*. A slightly refined method of comparison involves calculating a dollars-per-employee figure for each current contributor and using that statistic as a basis for evaluating new prospects or for requesting significant increases from old prospects. These statistics should be compiled separately for each major category and by size of firm (for example, heavy industrial manufacturers employing more than 5,000 people; service industries employing 50-100 people) because the variances among groups may be significant.

   The resultant figure can often be used as a strong selling point ("Isn't it worth seventy-five cents a person to have such a high quality of life in our area?"), especially if connected with contribution incentives such as discount tickets or memberships. If no other information is available, one may multiply the number of employees by an arbitrary figure, such as a dollar, and ask for that amount.

   The drawbacks of this method are similar to those of the general comparative method men-

8

tioned above. In addition, the employee information required may not be readily available. This method is particularly useful for manufacturing facilities; it is not very useful for evaluating corporate headquarters located in the area because they usually contribute disproportionately large amounts compared to their employment size.

4. *Formula.* A statistical approach to evaluation is based on the Filer Commission's recommendation that corporations give 2 percent of their pretax net income to charitable causes (see *Giving in America*, Report of the Commission on Private Philanthropy and Public Needs, 1975, p. 21). This figure can be obtained for each company on the list by multiplying its total revenue figure by the average pretax net income percentage for its particular industry (two sources for these data are *Business Week* and the U.S. Department of Commerce) and the result by 2 percent. This amount constitutes the total charitable giving level as recommended by the Filer Commission.

To ascertain what portion of the total should be contributed to arts and culture, one may apply a percentage for this category derived by the Conference Board, multiplying it by the figure obtained above (see Conference Board Report#694, *Annual Survey of Corporate Contributions*, New York: Conference Board, Inc.).

Although in many respects this method of evaluation is the most objective and rational of the six presented here, its use may present several problems. First, it may be difficult to obtain the statistics needed for each company. Second, although the Filer Commission's percentage is a target, the Conference Board's figures are averages and therefore historical, not forward-looking. Third, this method generates a "gross" statistic: the figures are for an entire company, without allowances for how the company's contributions are divided among the various geographic areas in which the company has facilities. Also, the Conference Board's arts and culture figure may include capital contributions and other special gifts, not just an arts council contribution. However, tendencies toward over statement can be partially mitigated by applying the formula to current large givers and developing a discount factor that allows for these considerations.

5. *United Way*. According to American Council for the Arts, corporate arts giving in some areas averages 20 percent of United Way giving. Therefore, a company might be asked for an amount equal to a percentage of its United Way contribution.

This approach does provide a good general guideline, especially if used in conjunction with one or more of the other evaluation methods. Often, however, United Way data are unattainable. Furthermore, this method assumes that 20 percent is the proper figure for arts giving.

6. *Arbitrary assessment*. When all else fails, guess! Although this is the least desirable course in terms of both accuracy and justifiability, it may

be the only method available for certain firms—
especially for small ones of a type never before
approached. Developing ascending categories
according to gift size provides a rationale for asking certain amounts from such arbitrarily
evaluated companies.

Once the evaluation of the prospect list has been
completed, the list should be sorted by evaluation amount to
determine quickly who the key prospects are. Typically, 10 or
20 corporations will provide well over three-quarters of the
total amount expected. An analysis by SIC code will reveal
significant industries and indicate whether or not a special approach for them is warranted.

Additionally, whenever possible the committee should
verify that the individuals noted on the list are the proper contacts. Committee members may also suggest possible solicitors.

The evaluation committee is not only an effective
way to arrive at request sizes, but its use is generally acceptable
to businesses, whose representatives often ask how their company's contribution level was determined.

PRODUCT DEVELOPMENT AND PACKAGING

Once potential "customers" have been specifically identified, the broad, composite characteristics of this market and its needs should be analyzed, and a product and marketing approach developed to meet them. For corporations to contribute to a fund drive, they must first be persuaded of the value of the endeavors they are being asked to support. In the case of an arts council fund drive, the arts (and the council as a funding vehicle) comprise the product that must be sold to the business world.

In general, companies and company executives are results-oriented. They are interested in what a product or service will achieve. They are spending money that belongs to their stockholders and they are responsible for seeing that it is used wisely. They are particularly interested in what specific impact the product in question will have on employees, the community, and thus, their business. In short, they want returns on their contribution investment.

An important adjunct to this point is often completely ignored by arts organizations. Corporations want to support something that is positive and growing. People — and companies are people — want to invest in something good, not something failing. They want to back a winner. The argument that the arts should be supported because they are dying is extremely negative and should never be used. How much better and more compelling it is to say: "The arts are doing rich and exciting things; they need your support to do them!"

Since corporate executives are accustomed to businesslike methods, fund raising should be on a businesslike basis. The presentation should be concise, factual, and supported by statistics wherever possible. Above all, it should be brief and focused; it should be clear, with a minimum of technical verbiage and a maximum of short, direct statements.

In general, business executives feel that arts organizations are poorly managed. This assumption must be counteracted. Thus, an important ingredient in a presentation consists of statistics, facts, or approaches that demonstrate that the arts and the arts council are being well-run.

An important caveat must be mentioned, however. At no time should the approach or presentation be anything but direct and truthful. Selling is presenting the product in a truthful fashion with emphasis on the points that will be particularly appealing to the prospective customer. For example, a small company in a small town may have no interest in what an arts council is doing in a community 40 miles away. What will appeal most to that proprietor is what the arts council is doing for the immediate area. The latter, therefore, is what should be emphasized in the presentation made to that company, even if the council is serving both areas.

Written Analyses

Too often, arts councils and arts organizations fail to describe themselves in terms that are both clear and appealing to their markets. One way in which a businesslike presentation can be developed is to begin with a complete written analysis containing all salient facts and arguments. Such a comprehensive document will clarify the philosophy and direction of the organization's endeavors. Moreover, everything else can be related to it—summaries and slogans for use in advertising can be derived from it; programs and projects will stem from its plans. Anyone who wants to learn about the arts council and its activities will thus have a comprehensive, yet succinct, source of information.

An arts council is only as important as the arts it supports. Therefore, in developing a written analysis of the arts council, the starting point is a clear description of what the organization means when it refers to the "arts."

"The arts" is a vague phrase, often not clearly grasped by either user or listener. It is important for business executives—or anyone else for that matter—to be able to identify clearly what is meant by "the arts" if they are to fund them. For an arts council, this can be a relatively simple matter: "the arts" can mean those organizations receiving or about to receive support. Large organizations may be cited by name, others by type of endeavor. In Greater Hartford, for example, the arts organizations consist of a major art museum, theater, ballet company, opera, symphony and chamber orchestra, in addition to a number of community arts groups and festivals.

A brief description of the specific arts events or activities and of the artistic excellence of local organizations is important in order to generate a feeling of pride in the high caliber of groups requiring support. Quotations from news-papers, such as the *New York Times*, or nationally renowned critics are useful in this context.

In addition, any favorable analysis of the managerial excellence of the arts organizations can be used here. For ex-ample, administrative costs may have increased only 2 percent over the past year, or as is the case with Hartford's major groups, local organizations may be earning a higher percent-age of their operating budgets than the national average. (The Ford Foundation has published national statistics in *The Fi-nances of the Performing Arts,* New York, 1974.) The pres-ence of top business leaders on a board is often taken as a good indicator of a well-run organization

Clear statements on the importance of the arts to the community should be developed. The involvement in the arts of a large segment of the population should be stressed. All statements should be buttressed by facts and statistics, both local and national.

Exhibit D contains major arguments for supporting the arts developed by the Greater Hartford Arts Council.

The fact that the arts cannot become self-sufficient is well known in most arts circles but hardly at all outside them. The level of costs for the arts is set by the general economy, where productivity improvements can be instituted to offset price increases. But such improvements are not possi-ble for the arts: a play or symphony written 200 years ago still has to be handcrafted, still requires the same number of per-formers as it did then. To increase admission charges to make them commensurate with costs not only would limit public ac-cess to the arts but would tend to be self-defeating, because such prices would be far above what many people would be willing to pay. Contributors, then, must make up the differ-ence between costs and earned revenues. (For analyses of the economic state of the arts see the Ford Foundation's *The Finances of the Performing Arts*, and William J. Baumol and William G. Bowen, *Performing Arts: The Economic Dilemma*, New York: The Twentieth Century Fund, 1966, ch. VII.)

After the arts themselves have been described, a written analysis of the arts council and its importance to the arts should be developed. This analysis should include the following sections:

1. *Definition.* The first section should be a general description of the arts council in two or three paragraphs. It should contain the council's basic objectives or charter.

2. *History and current events.* A one- or two-page summary of the arts council's major accomplishments is important as a record of achievements and even more so as an indication of the council's ability to fulfill its plans. A detailed analysis of sources and uses of funds may be presented either here or separately in an annual report.

3. *Long-range goals.* The four or five major accomplishments the arts council wishes to achieve over the next five years should be outlined. Like every other aspect of the arts council's activities, the goals must be consistent with the general objectives stated in the first part.

4. *Plan of action.* The specific projects and programs to be undertaken during the next year in order to achieve the long-range goals should be detailed, along with their expected costs and benefits.

5. *Reasons for support.* The last section should

summarize the reasons why funds should be given to an arts council rather than directly to the arts organizations themselves. Key points may be:

- that the council's appeal for funds represents a united, federated approach to giving and that corporations will not be approached separately by the organizations supported by the council
- that the arts council supplies unique services to the arts, such as in-kind assistance, central coordination, and similar services
- that because of the arts council's activities, dollars given to it can have an impact on the arts far beyond the face value of the donation — in short, there is a "multiplier" or "leverage" effect
- that the council's budget review committees help ensure that the arts are being well managed and that contributions are going where they can do the most good

Visual and Written Presentations

With the written analyses of the arts and the arts council as a base, visual and written presentations can be prepared.

A 10- to 15-minute visual presentation should be developed for use before corporate contributions committees. This presentation should contain a brief description of the arts, their value and importance, the economic problem, and highlights of the arts council's achievements and plans. It should include a place for mentioning the specific amount being requested of the particular corporation. An effective technique used by the Greater Hartford Arts Council was to combine slides with a written script. Flip charts and other visual exhibits are also useful. A slightly different version of the slide show may be developed for use before a more general audience, such as a service club.

The costs for such a presentation can be minimal. Slides may be obtained from arts groups; others can be made up. A corporate public relations department in an advertising firm may be helpful in developing this presentation. (However, caution should be exercised, as it is difficult to ask someone to revise what was done free of charge.)

In some cases a written presentation is preferable to a personal one. For this purpose, a one- or two-page letter should be prepared which outlines the basic reasons for supporting the arts and ends with a specific request for funds. The letter should be accompanied by key materials, including the full written analyses developed previously. Exhibit E is a presentation letter used by the Greater Hartford Arts Council.

Special approaches or targeted arguments should be developed wherever necessary. Key phrases or figures can then be inserted in the standard presentation for particular companies. For example, in a presentation to a company in an outlying region, a statement may be included on the popularity of the arts in that region, citing how many people from that particular area participate.

In addition to visual and written presentations designed for general use, detailed analyses of all arts council programs and operations should be made. A line-item budget should be drawn up. Additionally, administrative expenses should be shown according to activity, to indicate the prorated costs of fund raising, information coordination, in-kind services, and so forth. (See Charles A. Nelson and Frederick J. Turk, *Financial Management for the Arts*, New York: ACA, 1975, for an excellent explanation of this procedure.) These data are especially important for showing fund raising expenses as a percentage of total funds raised. Such materials, prepared in a clear and concise format, along with any major policy statements, should be made available on request.

CAMPAIGN STRATEGY

Once the market has been identified and the "product" has been developed and packaged, the broad strategy for the campaign can be outlined. This strategy includes the use of solicitors for personal contact with prospects and the division of the campaign into two phases, as well as attention to the uses of publicity during the campaign.

Personal Approach

The best approach in fund raising is direct personal contact. And the most effective personal approach is by someone who either knows the individual making the contribution decision or who can influence that individual. If, as is usually the case, such a solicitor is unavailable for each prospect, the next best step is to conduct a brief face-to-face interview with the company contact.

Overloading solicitors can result in calls being poorly made; therefore, a solicitor should be asked to see no more than five prospects.

Two-Phase Campaign

The campaign should be divided into two basic phases: the major corporations phase and the general campaign.

The timing of the major corporations phase will depend on when each company makes its contributions decision. For corporations on a calendar fiscal year, this phase will probably occur between September and November. Because the top 30 prospects on the list will probably provide 75 percent or more of the campaign's total receipts, they should be handled on a personal, "custom" basis. As soon as possible, the company should be contacted to find out when the contributions decision will be made. One can usually find out who is involved in contributions by a phone call to the company or one of its corporate officers. The person in charge of contributions should be asked about the decision date and whether it will be possible to make a brief personal presentation to the contributions committee.

Influential board members or business leaders participating in the fund drive should be used in the major corporations phase of the campaign. They should actually make the presentations, with the head of the professional staff accompanying them.

All other companies on the prospect list should be approached during the general campaign. This segment of the drive should begin with an official "kick-off" date and should last two months. An additional month should be allowed for "mop-up" activities. The campaign should be held when it does not conflict with any other major fund drive, such as the United Way.

Normally, solicitors in the general campaign should not be "big name" individuals but rather upper-middle-level managers with the time and ambition to devote themselves to the task.

Publicity

For a business-only campaign, publicity is helpful as an indirect reinforcement. By making individuals more aware of the arts and the arts council, publicity tends to get more company employees involved in the arts. Articles on fund-drive leaders and captains are useful vehicles for expressing appreciation to volunteers and reinforcing their enthusiasm. In addition, general publicity is useful during the campaign for motivating solicitors.

However, because companies and not individuals are being solicited, publicity and promotion are not integral to the campaign; in fact, a corporate-only campaign could conceivably be conducted without any strong media support. Thus publicity is not useful enough to warrant a significant outlay of money.

Press releases, feature articles, and public service announcements on radio and TV are often produced by individuals and run by broadcast stations on a volunteer basis. Whatever kinds of publicity are used they should both precede and continue into the general campaign phase.

A good form of promotion consists of speeches before service clubs, chambers of commerce, and similar organizations primarily made up of business executives. Such talks should be scheduled both during the campaign and throughout the year.

ORGANIZATION

An effective fund raising campaign requires a high degree of organization of personnel and materials. Primary responsibility for the successful operation of the fund drive rests with the professional staff and the executive director, who must provide the day-to-day leadership. The professional staff provide 99 percent of the work — the backup to the efforts of the volunteer solicitors. The staff organizes, follows up, makes phone calls, and so forth. (A large staff is not, however, a prerequisite for managing such a campaign. At the Greater Hartford Arts Council, four professional staff handled the 1977 fund drive as well as all other aspects of the council's operation.)

Structure

Exhibit F shows an organization chart for a corporate fund drive. Exhibit G contains brief job descriptions prepared for the Greater Hartford Arts Council's 1977 fund drive.

Honorary Chairperson. This position (or positions) is entirely optional. A prominent business executive or national figure can lend prestige to the campaign because such an individual's participation indicates endorsement of the drive's goals. Often, honorary chairpersons are not asked to do any work nor are they required to appear at meetings.

Chairperson. The chair must be a strong and influential business leader. This person will actually run the campaign and act as the final arbiter of any decisions concerning it. If possible, this position should have a two-year term.

Having a strong and hard-working volunteer fund-drive chairperson, as we had in Hartford, can have a very positive impact on the campaign. However, securing a good leader is not always possible, so the campaign should be organized to minimize negative effects of having a poor chairperson.

Vice-Chairperson. As chairperson-elect, this individual should have the same qualities as the chair.

Steering Committee. This is an optional group made up of prestigious leaders who supervise captains and work out strategies.

Captains. A captain's role is to lead and monitor a team of 10 or 15 solicitors. Therefore, the captain should be a strong leader, attentive to detail and dedicated to getting the solicitors to finish their assignments as quickly and effectively as possible.

The team may be organized to deal with specific industries (for example, a team for soliciting law firms) or on a general basis, where each team may cover a variety of firms. Circumstances dictate which may be the most effective or whether some combination of the two types is appropriate. (In 1977, the Greater Hartford Arts Council had 18 teams organized along general lines.)

Solicitors. These are the individuals who actually call on the prospects. For the general campaign, in which small firms form the bulk of the prospects, relatively young, middle-management executives often have more time, energy, and ambition to work as solicitors than do top corporate executives. Younger executives may be especially inspired if the board of the fund-drive organization contains chief executives from their firms.

Recruitment

There are two basic ways of using volunteers: Get a few to do a lot of work or get many, each to do a little work. With the former approach, 20 to 30 executives might be loaned to work full time during the course of the campaign. On leave from their companies, they would do nothing else but solicit. The problem with this approach is that it involves a heavy investment on the part of the companies, one they may be reluctant to make. In Hartford, the latter approach was used and is the one described below.

Recruiting volunteers for the fund drive can be one of the most time-consuming and burdensome of tasks. Obtaining the "name" individuals to serve in the highest positions should be done either by the board of directors or by the fund-drive chairperson. For the balance of positions — usually all the captains and solicitors — the professional staff must do most of the recruiting. An average day may involve more than 40 telephone calls, half of which are never completed, because people are not at their desks, or they are in a meeting, and so forth. In fact, three calls may be required on the average to reach each person. Of those who are contacted, approximately half agree to help with the campaign.

The number of prestigious business leaders needed depends on the number of major firms to be solicited and the number of top fund-drive positions that need to be filled. In 1977, the Greater Hartford Arts Council approached 30 major corporations. Ten required written presentations, 20 were solicited personally by the fund drive chairperson and by other members of the arts council board.

Because the maximum number of prospects assigned to each solicitor is five, the minimum number of solicitors needed is the total number of prospects divided by five. Enough captains are needed to organize solicitors into teams of 10 to 15 each. In 1977, the Greater Hartford Arts Council solicited 960 companies using 18 captains and 200 solicitors.

The council should recruit 10 percent more solicitors than are needed so that individuals who are not performing their tasks can be replaced immediately. These "extras" should be involved in the campaign at the outset; they should be given one or two prospects, with the understanding that they may receive additional assignments later in the campaign.

If the council cannot obtain the required number of solicitors, it should reduce the number of prospects accordingly to maintain the ratio of five prospects per solicitor. Reducing the number of prospects will have a minimal financial effect on the campaign if the smallest firms are removed from the list. The alternative of increasing the number of prospects per solicitor is unacceptable, especially because many of these same solicitors will be needed for next year's drive.

Three groups of people comprise core sources of information about, or suggestions for, solicitors: arts council board members, boards of beneficiaries, and past solicitors. The evaluation committee may also generate names of potential solicitors. Promotion notices in local papers or company newsletters may bring forward interested persons. In short, any list of names to which "cold" calls can be made can be utilized.

An effective approach to a prospective solicitor involves an appeal to community spirit, an emphatic guarantee that no more than five prospects will be assigned for solicitation, and assurance of all the organizational support and information necessary to do the job in a minimum amount of time. It is extremely helpful also to mention key executives from the person's own firm who are already involved in the council's drive. A brief thank-you note confirming the agreement and conditions should be sent once an individual has agreed to take part.

Fund-drive workers should be trained. If possible, each solicitor should attend a session given by a sales training professional. If that is impossible, other training devices, such as tapes or written materials developed with the aid of a professional, can be used. In any case, training should include some exposure to the activities and facilities of the major beneficiaries.

As soon as possible after recruitment, the professional staff should assign 10 to 15 solicitors to a team. Care should be taken to ensure that the teams are as balanced as possible, so that, for example, strong and weak solicitors are on each team and that potentially weak captains have strong solicitors. Once the solicitors are assigned to teams, the staff should check the rosters with the respective captains before confirming the assignments to the solicitors.

Prospect Assignment

Ideally every solicitor should look over the entire list and pick the prospects he or she wants to solicit. However, in a large fund raising campaign such a procedure is impractical. An effective alternative is to assign prospects to specific teams rather than to individual solicitors. The staff goes through the entire prospect list and assigns companies to teams according to the following criteria:

- a past contributor is assigned to a team that includes that company's past solicitor
- new or old prospects are assigned to teams that include, in the following order of priority, (1) a solicitor identified by the evaluation committee; (2) the company's executive or senior officer; (3) an executive of a firm in the same field, or (4) a solicitor living or working in the same area as the prospective donor.

The balance of the prospects can be assigned arbitrarily to each team until its quota of prospects is filled. In making assignments, the staff should be careful to see that good and bad, new and old, prospects are evenly distributed. Having many problem prospects can greatly discourage individual solicitors and the team.

At the first team meeting, the list of prospects assigned to the team is reviewed by each team member. Each solicitor then selects the five prospects he wishes to solicit. Those left after all known prospects are assigned should be parcelled out arbitrarily.

PRECAMPAIGN ACTIVITES

Other activities that must take place before the campaign begins include revising the schedule of weekly tasks and responsibilities, and if necessary the duration of tasks; setting the campaign goal; determining how the funds would be allocated to beneficiaries if the total goal were met; instituting campaign incentives; and preparing and distributing campaign materials.

Setting the Campaign Goal

The overall goal for the fund drive should be based on a realistic estimate of the amount that can be raised. A figure representing the total needs of arts groups can be used in the sales presentation, but not as the basis for the campaign goal. Too low a campaign goal provides too little incentive; too high a goal will result in "failure," which could have a negative impact long after the close of the campaign.

A rational way of establishing the campaign target employs probabilities. If, for example, the staff or the evaluation committee determines that the chances of obtaining the full amount requested from all new prospects are only 10 out of 100, the "expected value" for new prospect evaluations is the total target times 10 percent.

In 1977, the Greater Hartford Arts Council raised more than $529,000 from the business community. Based on an analysis of contributions during this campaign, a conservative and realistic method of establishing the fund drive goal was arrived at, involving three asumptions:

- past contributors will give at least the same amount they did the previous year. For Hartford this was a reasonable assumption since the attrition rate was under 1 percent; in other areas, a discounted figure may be necessary to allow for attrition
- the probability of obtaining the full amount of increases requested from all past contributors is 40 percent
- the chance of getting the full request from all new prospects is 15 percent

Thus, the campaign goal can be calculated by adding the two figures derived from the following formulas:

Past contributors: (100% × total raised in past drive) + (40% × requested increase) = total expected from past contributors

New prospects: 15 % × total evaluation = total expected from new prospects

The sum of these two figures can then be rounded upwards or downwards as circumstances dictate.

For example, using this method a council would arrive at a campaign goal in the following way.

- The council raised $400,000 in the previous year (1976); its evaluations committee, working on the assumption that past contributors would contribute the same or more to the 1977 campaign, examined each past contributor and estimated the amount of the increase to be asked of each. The requested increases totaled $100,000, bringing the evaluation for past contributors to $500,000.

- The evaluations committee then examined new prospects and, totaling the individual evaluations, arrived at an evaluation for new prospects of $200,000.

Applying the formula outlined above:

Past contributors:

Total raised in past drive
$400,000 × 100% $400,000

Requested increases for 1977
$100,000 × 40%   40,000

Total expected from past contributors   *$440,000*

New Prospects:
Total evaluation $200,000 × 15%   30,000

Total expected from new prospects   *$ 30,000*

Goal for 1977 fund drive   *$470,000*

Determining Preliminary Allocations

Before soliciting corporations, a preliminary allocation of the expected total must be made in order to show prospective donors how their contributions will be used. This allocation can be made by category (for example, performing arts), or by organization (for example, Hartford Ballet), or by a combination of both, where major institutions are identified and small groups are combined into one or two categories.

Naturally, designated beneficiaries must be cautioned about the preliminary nature of their allocations and that the amount of the final award cannot be determined until the fund drive is over.

Developing Contribution Incentives

If possible, contribution incentives should be developed and included in the presentation. Some of the most frequently used are:

Challenge grants. A funding agency's challenge grant, which matches new or total money raised, is perhaps the most effective incentive. By its very nature such a grant greatly enhances the impact or "buying power" of each contributor's gift. A special case of such a grant is that in which the top 10 corporations in an area match the new money raised from small businesses.

Employee benefits. Corporate memberships or discount tickets for employees of donor companies can be excellent contribution incentives. Such benefits can be given at little or no cost to arts groups, particularly if they involve events such as previews, which would not be sold out anyway.

Recognition. "Image" and recognition are very im-- portant to many corporations. All contributors should be listed in arts council publications such as the annual report. (Additionally, including the names of solicitors in council publications will enhance their motivation.) Major beneficiaries may be willing to advertise the top donors in their printed programs. Incentives and benefits should be offered throughout the entire year for maximum impact.

Distributing Campaign Materials

Among the campaign materials that solicitors must have at kick-off time are the prospect list, the written analyses of the arts and the arts council, and supplemental materials.

The list of five prospects given to each solicitor must be accurate and complete. Nothing is more frustrating than to call an incorrect number or a wrong contact, or to have inaccurate information about previous contributions.

A solicitor must know about the arts and the council in order to promote their worth. Therefore, each solicitor should receive and become familiar with the written documents describing the activities and worth of organizations supported by the council, as well as the council itself. In addition, solicitors should see the slide presentation, which reinforces the highlights of these materials. Moreover, seeing the slide presentation also acquaints solicitors with its availability for use in the campaign.

A packet of information given to the solicitors at the kick-off meeting completes the materials they should receive. The kit should contain answers to anticipated questions, contact and selling hints, and any necessary details about the prospects to be approached. Exhibit H is a sample solicitor kit.

Holding Team Meetings

During the month preceding the kick-off, each fund-drive captain should hold a team meeting. The purposes of this meeting are to provide solicitors with basic information on the arts and the arts council; to enable solicitors to select prospects from those assigned to their team; and to acquaint team members with one another and their captain in order to develop team consciousness.

A team meeting should last no more than an hour and should be conducted by the team captain, although the meeting may be based on comprehensive staff work, which may even include developing a written script and an outline of the meeting for the captain's use.

The schedule, details, and, especially, the deadlines of the general campaign should be impressed upon solicitors at this time. Information on selling techniques should also be presented.

A dollar goal should be set for each team in the same way the overall goal was established. Naturally, the sum of all team goals must equal the target for the whole drive.

Prizes for the team and individual efforts should be mentioned during this meeting. For example, concert series tickets may be awarded to the top fund-raising team, or memberships in a local art museum. Prizes may also be awarded to encourage particular directions in fund raising such as awarding a prize to the person or team soliciting the largest percentage of new money.

After the initial meeting, the captain should write a brief note to each team member.

THE CAMPAIGN

Major Corporations Campaign

One phase of the fund drive occurs when the targeted corporations make their contributions decisions, usually in the last quarter of the calendar year.

Wherever possible, an influential board member or fund-drive volunteer should make a personal presentation to the contributions committee using the written script and slide presentation developed previously. At the end of the presentation, the presentor should give the head of the committee a letter making the official contributions request, the basic documents on the arts council, and any additional materials requested by the committee.

Unless a specific decision date has been indicated, the committee head may be telephoned in four to six weeks to see whether additional information is needed and to learn when the decision will be made.

General Campaign

About three days before the kick-off meeting, the arts council president, fund drive chairperson, or honorary chairperson should send an individual letter to each prospect. One type of letter should be sent to new prospects, another to past contributors. Those used by the Greater Hartford Arts Council in 1977 are shown in Exhibit I.

The letter should introduce the arts council, its fund drive, and the caliber of individuals involved in it; highlight the basic reasons for supporting the drive; and act as a "door-opener" for solicitors (who can then approach the prospect with something like, "I'm calling to follow up on Walter Connolly's letter of January 12...").

The general campaign should open with a brief, well-organized kick-off meeting that lasts an hour or less. Such an event not only marks the official beginning of the drive, but also brings solicitors to one place so that final materials can be distributed. Most importantly, it should provide a high degree of motivation and stimulus to the solicitors.

All solicitors, captains, and other fund-drive workers, arts council board members, representative individuals from arts organizations, and the press should be present. The presence of especially prominent business executives and dignitaries may provide an added incentive for attendance. Moreover, one way to obtain free publicity is to have important figures, such as the mayor or governor, address the group.

The primary stimulus, however, will be the very presence, in one place, of all solicitors and arts council supporters. This stimulus can be reinforced if the meeting is well managed and interesting. Such kick-offs add to the conviction of fund-drive workers that they are part of a well-run, highly efficient and effective operation that will be successful.

Despite all the organization and motivation provided solicitors, they are often sidetracked by daily problems and special circumstances. The key to fund-drive success is quick, decisive action. Faltering solicitors will rarely, if ever, take action on their own. Thus the general campaign requires monitoring, follow-up, and pressure.

Ideally, solicitors should be contacted by their captain, captains by steering committee members, or the fund-drive chairperson, on a weekly basis. These contacts should be supplemented by telephone calls from the professional staff.

One week after the kick-off, each captain and solicitor should be called by the professional staff to find out what is happening, whether anything is needed, or whether there are special problems. Note should be made of solicitors who do not seem to be doing anything or will not return calls. Any solicitor who has not started work after two weeks should be dropped and the prospects reassigned, unless there was an exceptionally good reason for lack of action that no longer applies. If the captain does not make these reassignments, the professional staff should. There is no need for the staff to be apologetic or hesitant about such actions. Each solicitor has agreed to help and has made a commitment to perform a specific task. As long as the staff has done its job of providing information and support, the volunteer has no excuse for not following through.

The team captains should meet every other week, starting two weeks after the kick-off. At these meetings, each captain should report on the team's accomplishments: prospects contacted and dollars raised. There should also be discussion of common problems and suggestions on their solution.

If possible a newsletter should be sent out to all fund-drive workers after each report meeting. Such a letter will keep all workers informed and motivated. It should summarize progress to date and outline special techniques or suggested solutions to common problems.

During the third week of the campaign, captains should meet with their teams. The purpose and content of these meetings are the same as those of the captains' meetings. They are also the first face-to-face contacts between captains and solicitors since the beginning of the campaign.

If it can be arranged, a maximum amount of publicity should be generated during the general campaign, especially in its first month. News releases, public service announcements, and similar promotional items are helpful in increasing general awareness of the drive and in providing reinforcement to solicitors.

Almost inevitably, some prospects will not have made a decision by the end of the campaign. Board meetings may not have occurred during the campaign period, or reassignments among solicitors and other delays may have extended the solicitation period. An extra month after the campaign's official end should be allowed, therefore, for "mopup." Unless significant contributions are still pending, the campaign should be shut off after that period. Any stragglers should be left for next year's drive.

POSTCAMPAIGN ACTIVITIES

Proper follow-up and review after the conclusion of the campaign are important for the success of next year's efforts.

Personal thank-you letters should be sent to all contributors as soon as possible after their gifts are received. At the conclusion of the campaign, or as soon as their assignments have been completed, all fund-drive workers should receive special thank-you letters. Letters to both contributors and solicitors may come from the president, the fund-drive chairperson, or the honorary chairperson.

Beneficiaries and major grant recipients may also want to write directly to top contributors and fund-drive workers to express their appreciation.

After the conclusion of the campaign each fund-drive worker should be interviewed and asked to indicate the strong and weak points of the campaign and how the campaign might be improved. Solicitors can also provide updated information about their prospects. The solicitor may suggest that certain prospects be removed from the list. This should be done only if there is no chance they will ever be induced to contribute. The names of such prospects should be coded in a special way and noted on a separate list. At the outset of the next fund drive, this list should be shown to every solicitor to see if any has influence with any of these "hard-core" cases. If not, they should be approached by a special team, by the professional staff, or not at all.

The good work of both contributors and solicitors can be reinforced in a variety of ways. Lists of all contributors should be drawn up, both alphabetically and by type of business. These should be sent to all fund-drive workers and board members with the suggestion that the next time they do business with a contributor they express their gratitude for support of the arts council. Special invitations or privileged seating at special events are also effective ways of showing appreciation to both contributors and solicitors.

The critical aspect of the reinforcement process is continued communication. Throughout the year, contributors and solicitors should be informed of special activities and accomplishments of both the arts and the arts council. For example, a month or so after the campaign's conclusion, details on the total raised and how it was distributed should be sent to council supporters. Releases on special awards received by arts groups may also be sent out by the arts council.

As soon as the last detail of the current campaign is completed, preparations should begin for next year's efforts. Suggested improvements should be made and information updated. Then the process described begins again.

PLANNING AND IMPLEMENTATION

The planning and implementation of a fund drive along the lines of the campaign described above may be undertaken in the following sequence of steps.

1. *Review.* The first step is for council directors and professional staff to review the current procedures for corporate fund drives. They should begin to look at what features of the recommended campaign plan are already in place, and what changes will have to be made. The concepts and techniques described above are broadly applicable to every kind of council. But adaptations may be required to fit particular circumstances.

2. *Set goals.* Targets should be set for the number and kind of prospects to be approached in the forthcoming campaign. These goals are arrived at by examining such questions as whether the number of prospects should be increased, or kept the same but approached more effectively; whether lawyers and doctors should be approached this year, or just industry. Even though the goals may be tentative at this time, it is important to set them because doing so gives direction and focus to campaign planning.

3. *Determine requirements.* The next step is to

identify exactly what will be needed to make the desired changes and to achieve the desired goals. Because the primary constraint is time, a rough schedule of activities should be drawn up immediately and then translated into a week-by-week list of tasks (see Exhibit A). This process is time-consuming but essential, for it will clearly show what has to be done and what time and personnel will be required.

Once the campaign program as outlined looks feasible, and all its components have been scheduled, start on it —adhering as closely as possible to the schedule.

Above all, do well whatever you have chosen to do. Excellence and success create a substantial base for the future.

LIST OF EXHIBITS

CALENDAR OF EVENTS

Date	Description
April 15	End of current fund drive
April 16-May 15	Review with solicitors Institute improvements
May 16-July 15	Develop prospect list and evaluation
July 16-August 15	Develop presentation
August 16-September 15	Review strategy Set campaign goal Make preliminary allocations Recruit fund-drive workers
September 16-November 15	Major corporations drive
November 16-December 15	Develop campaign materials Assign prospects to teams Recruit fund-drive workers
December 16-January 15	Hold team meetings Assign prospects to solicitors Finish campaign materials
January 15	Kick-off meeting
January 15-March 15	General campaign
March 16-April 15	"Mop up"

FUND DRIVE SCHEDULE
SAMPLE PAGE

Date		Description	Allocation of Time (Hrs.)			
Week of	Day	Assigned to:	W G B	PM	LK / KF	MSL
10/11	11	Prospect research compilation	2	10	5	
	12	Prepare campaign materials	5	30	5	
	*13	3rd publicity mtg.: Prelim. design				
		& placement schedule	2	4	2	
		Corporate presentation	10	5		10
10/18	*18	MSL meeting	3	5	2	3
		Publicity meeting follow-up	1	4	2	
		Mail campaign update	1	4	2	
		Finalize campaign materials		5	2	
10/25	27	Computer status report	1			
	28	Sustained beneficiary mtg.: review				
		campaign materials	2	3	3	
	29	Finalize major fund proposals		10	2	
11/1	1	Solicitor assignments	2	8	2	
	3	Prospect research compilation ends	5	15	5	
11/8		Solicitor assignments	1	6	2	
	*	4th Vice-chmn. mtg.	2	3	4	2
11/15	15	Update prospect list (11/15 − 11/29)		2	3	
		Solicitor assignments	2	6	2	
11/22		Update prospect list			3	
	*	4th publicity mtg.: finalize				
		placement schedule	2	4	2	
11/29		Update prospect list (11/15 − 11/29)	1	2	3	
		Complete solic. recruitment &				
		assignment	2	20	5	
		Sub-total	44	146	56	15

OUT-OF-POCKET FUND-RAISING EXPENSES
(Greater Hartford Arts Council, 1977 Campaign)

Printing (including Annual Report and decals)	$2,000
Postage	1,500
Supplies & Services (including typing, envelopes, etc.)	1,000
Advertising*	15
Miscellaneous	250
	$4,765

---

* TV spots and other media coverage for the 1977 campaign were obtained without cost

Exhibit C

COMPUTERIZED PROSPECT LIST

The computerized prospect list for the Greater Hartford Arts Council's 1977 fund drive included basic data that were sorted and printed out in a variety of ways listed below. Schedule C-1 illustrates the format for the list sorted and printed by team captain and solicitor.

Version	Title	Description
1.	Master list	All data sorted alphabetically by company
2.	Team list	All data sorted by team, solicitor, and company. Printed one page per solicitor; pages then separated and given to each solicitor.
3.	Team summary	By team, solicitor, solicitor phone number, amount requested, contributions history. One line per prospect. One page per team. Used by captain.
4.	Geographic list	Company name and amount, sorted by town.
5.	Industry list	Company name and amount, sorted by SIC code.
6.	Evaluation list	Company name and amount, sorted by size of evaluation, in descending order.
7.	Labels	Program for properly printing contact name, company, and address on labels and pledge cards.
8.	Contributor list	Alphabetic list of company name only.

Exhibit C *(continued)*

Schedule C-1 Format
GREATER HARTFORD ARTS COUNCIL
1977 FUND DRIVE

Captain	Solicitor	Prospect	SIC	Acct.
Name	Name	Company	SIC	Acct.
Telephone	Telephone	Name	Code	No.
Number	Number	Address		

---

(1) Date on which contribution decision will be made.

(2) To be filled in with dollar amount when a pledge is received.

(3) To be filled in with dollar amount when the contribution is actually received.

Sales	Emp.	Date	Goal	Pledge	Paid	Lst yr	Prv yr
Sales ($ million)	No. of employees	(1)	1977 Target	(2)	(3)	(4)	(5)

---

(4) Last year's contribution history, coded to show, for example, the name of last year's solicitor, the approximate amount given or the refusal to give, and other such details.

(5) Previous year's contribution history, showing, for example amount given or refusal, etc.

NINE REASONS WHY BUSINESS SHOULD SUPPORT THE ARTS

First, it's good business:

1. Arts improve the quality of life. This makes it easier for companies to attract and keep good people.

2. The arts help bring tourists and conventions to Hartford.

3. Creativity is essential to business. Graphics and design are only the most obvious examples. The process of management is founded on creativity. A vital arts community provides the training and stimulus for creative people in all fields.

4. The arts comprise a $4 million local industry, employing hundreds of local people and providing substantial direct stimulus to the regional economy.

Second, the arts are important to society:

1. In a recent national survey 84% of the people interviewed thought that arts and cultural activities were as important for a community to have as "libraries, schools, parks, and recreational activities."*

2. They enrich our individual lives, whether we take lessons or go to concerts or merely experience the visual and performing arts of our area.

3. Our children have good teachers—for piano, for drawing, for all the fine arts—because there are good artists in our area, drawn to Greater Hartford by the vitality of our cultural climate.

4. The arts help the underprivileged. They ameliorate the brutality of an impersonal existence for the elderly, for the poor, for the disadvantaged of all kinds.

5. One of our richest assets is our cultural heritage; helping the arts increases the value of the heritage we leave for future generations.

---

* National Research Center of the Arts, *Americans and the Arts*, New York: ACA, 1976.

WRITTEN PRESENTATION LETTER

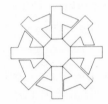

Greater Hartford Arts Council

W. Grant Brownrigg
Director

250 Constitution Plaza
Hartford, Connecticut 06103
(203) 525-8629

(Date)

(Name of Contact
Name of Corporation
Address)

Dear   :

The 1976-77 fund drive for the Greater Hartford Arts Council is underway. I am writing you to ask for your continued financial support so that together we can help maintain the unique quality of life in our area.

The Arts Council not only serves as a conduit for financial assistance to the arts, but it also provides a valuable review and challenge function. Through the volunteer efforts of a large group of business executives, administrative costs are being streamlined and marketing skills are being employed to attract larger audiences.

The recent Frank Sinatra Concert at the Civic Center was an artistic and financial success. We plan to have at least one more such event so that the combined proceeds will offset the entire administrative costs of the Arts Council. This would mean that 100% of every dollar contributed by the business community will go directly to the various arts organizations.

Specifically, we are asking that (Name of Corporation) consider carefully a contribution of $(amount) to the Greater Hartford Arts Council for its 1976-77 fund drive.

We'll be in touch with you in a few days to answer any questions not answered by this letter and the attached descriptive materials.

Sincerely,

(Name of Chairman)
Fund Campaign Committee Chairman

Enclosures (Enclose written analyses of arts/arts council background, importance, reasons for support.)

EXHIBIT F

FUND DRIVE ORGANIZATION CHART

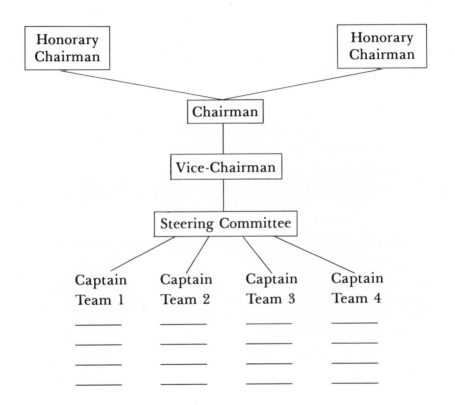

Exhibit G

FUND DRIVE JOB DESCRIPTIONS

I. **Chairman**

   A. **Precampaign**—Create fund drive organization.

      1. Recruit honorary co-chairmen.

      2. Identify and recruit chairman-elect.

      3. Help recruit captains.

      4. Develop organizational structure & reporting procedures.

   B. **Precampaign**—Solicit major contributors.

     Schedule and coordinate personal presentations.
     Use captains, board members as appropriate.

   C. **Campaign**—Act as general manager of campaign.

II. **Vice-Chairman**

   A. **Precampaign**—Head the evaluation committee. Evaluate prospects and assign solicitors with aid of captains.

   B. **Campaign**—Supervise three captains.

III. **Steering Committee Functions**

   A. Member One

      1. **Precampaign**—Create a strategy to inform and involve area service clubs (Rotary, Kiwanis, Lions, etc.).

      2. **Campaign**—Supervise four captains.

   B. Member Two

      1. **Precampaign**—Head a committee to oversee the development and implementation of a publicity strategy for the campaign.

      2. **Campaign**—Supervise four captains.

IV. **Captains**

      1. **Precampaign**—Hold organizational team meetings; help recruit solicitors as needed.

      2. **Campaign**—Supervise 10-15 solicitors; provide monitoring and motivation; help solve problems.

V. **Solicitors**

      1. **Precampaign**—Attend organizational team meeting, review materials, select prospects.

      2. **Campaign**—Solicit up to five prospects; report results and information.

Exhibit H

SAMPLE SOLICITOR KIT

This exhibit contains a sample of the materials given to each solicitor at the kick-off meeting of the Greater Hartford Arts Council's 1977 fund drive.

Schedule H-1 is the Table of Contents for both the solicitor kit and the other schedules.

Where available, articles on prospects were included in the appropriate solicitor's kit along with any other special information or facts that might be needed (such as the importance of the arts to a particular, remote town where a prospect is located).

TABLE OF CONTENTS

1977 FUND DRIVE
APPROACH & METHODOLOGY

I. Overall Approach

A. Soliciting contributions is very much like sales. Personal contact and product knowledge are the key ingredients.

    1. **Personal contact.** Please try to arrange for a personal visit to each prospect. Nothing is as effective as a face-to-face discussion, and your willingness to take time to do so shows your strong support of the Council's work.

    Also, it is essential that a prospective contributor know how valuable the arts are to the community. His awareness of their importance will have more beneficial results for the arts over the long term than a check written only to placate a solicitor.

    2. **Product knowledge.** Please read the materials provided you on the arts and the Arts Council so that you are well informed. If you need any further information, please call the staff (tel. no.).

B. Several important points to keep in mind.

    1. This is a "one-gift-for-the-arts" appeal; no other approach will be made this year.

    2. You are asking for an *investment* in the community, one that has high returns for business — not begging for a hand-out.

    3. Our local arts organizations are nationally renowned and have a far better earnings record than the U.S. average. Yet by their very nature, they are not able to support themselves.

II. Suggested Methodology

A. Contact your prospects the first day that you have your pledge cards.

    1. Refer to Walter Connolly's letter (copies enclosed).

2. Ask for an opportunity to discuss the Arts Council in a 10-15 minute personal interview (sample script enclosed).

3. You may wish to use one of the 3 sample letters enclosed as an initial "introduction" to be followed up by a telephone call or personal visit.

B. The Personal Interview.

1. Suggested outline is attached. It is based on the white paper, slide presentation, and other materials given each solicitor.

2. Try to "close the sale" at the time of the interview.

a. Fill out the pledge card and ask prospect to sign it, then you sign it.

3. Leave with the prospect.

a. Annual Report.

b. Copy of *Courant* article on Advocate Action Committee.

c. Decal.

4. Notify the Council if the prospect desires additional information.

C. Send thank you letter (sample attached). The Council will send an "official" thank you but a personal one from you would be important.

II. Procedures

A. Please contact your prospects and follow up as soon as possible. Quick action means the job is finished and out of the way with a minimum of effort.

1. Please fill out the Solicitor Report Form and send it in.

2. Self-addressed envelopes are provided for your use and that of your prospects.

B. The computer printout gives the best information that was available to the staff. Please verify this data wherever possible and note corrections and additions in the "Comments" column of the Report Form. All information will be invaluable for next year.

C. Tell your captain immediately if you're having problems with a prospect, so it can be reassigned if necessary.

Schedule H 3

SAMPLE TELEPHONE APPROACH

Solicitor: Hello my name is_____. Several days ago, Walter Connolly wrote to you about the Arts Council. I'm following up on his letter and would like 10 or 15 minutes of your time to talk with you about the Council.

Prospect: But I'm not interested in the arts!

Solicitor: I can understand that. Many of the businessmen who support the Council are not really interested in the arts themselves. They're interested in the *community*. Since the arts are important to the community, they feel it's important to support the arts. It's like investing money or buying inventory—you do it for the returns you expect to get, not for the sake of getting rid of your money.

Prospect: I don't have time to see you.

Solicitor: I'm only asking for 10 or 15 minutes. I'd like you to understand what we're doing. Even if you don't wish to contribute I'd like you to know about the arts and the Arts Council. I think it's important. That's why I'm calling you, that's why *I'm* taking the time to help the Council.

Prospect: Can't you do it over the phone?

Solicitor: No. It's important that I see you. I have information I'd like to show you. I'm only asking for 10 or 15 minutes.

Prospect: Can't you mail things to me?

Solicitor: It will actually take less time if I stop in and go over things with you for 10 or 15 minutes. I can give you the highlights and a good, overall understanding in that time, then leave information for you to peruse at your leisure.

Schedule H-4

SAMPLE SOLICITOR LETTER 1

Dear   :

As Walter Connolly pointed out in his recent letter
to you, the arts are very important to both business
and the community.

The Arts Council is currently conducting its annual
"one-gift-for-the-arts" fund drive. As one of the
solicitors for the drive, I will be in touch with you
in a few days to talk with you about our efforts.

Sincerely,

PERSONAL INTERVIEW OUTLINE

I. **Arts Council**
   A. Organized 5 years ago.
   B. Provides funds and in-kind services to arts groups in Greater Hartford.
   C. Endorsed by Chamber of Commerce.

II. **Arts Supported by Council**
   A. Six receive ongoing support:
      1. Wadsworth Atheneum
      2. Hartford Symphony
      3. Hartford Ballet Company
      4. Connecticut Opera
      5. Hartford Stage Company
      6. Hartford Chamber Orchestra
   B. Civic & Arts Festival
   C. Community Arts & Education groups like Artists Collective, Peace Train, and the North End Dance Troupe.

III. **State of Arts**
   A. Excellent quality.
   B. Better earnings ratio than the U.S. average.

IV. **Arts are important**
   A. To business
      1. Quality of life helps in recruiting.
      2. Tourists and conventions.
      3. Stimulates creativity in all areas.
      4. Direct economic impact ($4 million).
   B. To society
      1. Enrich individual lives.
      2. Good teachers for our children.
      3. Help to the underprivileged.
      4. Cultural heritage.

V. **Arts Council Activities**
   A. Fund Raising
      1. Corporations: "one-gift-for-the-arts".
      2. Private foundations.
      3. Special events (Sinatra concert, October 7).
   B. Strategic Planning
      1. Apply business techniques to increase revenue and decrease costs.
      2. Marketing plan to expand audiences.
   C. Improving assistance and coordination
      1. Advocate Action Committee Study: to see if any functions can be combined.
      2. Expanded in-kind services for any applicant arts group

VI. **Conclusion**
   A. Arts and Arts Council working hard to help themselves, but they can't do it alone. Need your support.
   B. Goal is $525,000. This is not the entire amount needed but a minimum necessary to enable groups to maintain essential services.
   C. Specifically, we are asking you to consider a contribution of $_____.

VII **Closing**
   1. (Ask prospect to sign pledge card.)
   2. (Leave Annual Report, *Courant* article, and decal.)
   3. Thank you.

ARTS ARE NOT JUST FOR THE ELITE FEW

I. **Survey Statistics**

   A. 84% of the people interviewed in a recent nationwide poll by Lou Harris agreed that "arts and cultural activities are as important for a community to have as libraries, schools, parks and recreational activities."

   B. According to a telephone survey of 618 people in Greater Hartford, 48% of the people with incomes of less than $10,000 per year and 45% of those with a high school education or less have made use of the Wadsworth Atheneum, for example.

II. **Arts Council Activities**

   A. All of the organizations receiving substantial funding from the Council have special programs to serve children, students, the poor and disadvantaged.

   B. In addition, the Council sponsors the annual Civic & Arts Festival on Constitution Plaza. It is entirely free and draws an estimated 100,000 people each year.

   C. The Council also provides substantial funding (over $50,000 in 1976) to small arts groups whose primary activities are in one or more of the following areas:

   . . . Education
   . . . Aid to the poor and disadvantaged
   . . . Service to young people
   . . . Programs for older adults

   This direct funding is in addition to the many hours of in-kind services provided these small groups by the Council staff as well as the Advocates Action Committee.

QUESTIONS & ANSWERS

I. **What is the quality of the arts in our area?**

Excellent. As examples:

A. The Hartford Stage Company's "All Over" was on public television in May 1976. It received excellent reviews by the *Wall Street Journal* and *New York Times*.

B. The Wadsworth Atheneum's collection of paintings contains works by almost every major artist — like Rembrandt, Trumbull, Picasso, and Wyeth — as well as one of five Caravaggios in the country.

C. The Hartford Symphony is second only to the Boston Symphony in New England. It puts on over 30 performances each year, including special concerts for students, ethnic groups and older adults.

D. The Hartford Ballet is the most active touring ballet company in America. In the spring of 1976, its leading dancer was a featured performer with the Joffrey in New York, to the rave reviews of New York papers.

E. The Connecticut Opera Association is the only professional opera company producing grand opera in Connecticut. In fact, it was the 13th professional company to be founded in this country.

F. The Hartford Chamber Orchestra has performed on WQXR in New York and with the Paul Taylor Dance Company at a world premiere in Newport.

II. **Can't the arts support themselves?**

No. The level of costs for the arts is set by the general economy, where productivity improvements can be instituted to offset increases. But such improvements are not possible for the arts — a play or symphony written 200 years ago still has to be handcrafted, still requires the same number of performers, as it did then.

Increasing admission charges commensurate with costs would not only limit public access to the arts but would also tend to be self-defeating, in that the resultant prices would be far above what people would be willing to pay.

The difference between costs and earned revenues must be made up by contributors.

III. **How do the arts in Hartford compare to the rest of the nation?**

Better. The major organizations in Hartford all earn a higher percentage of their operating budget than the national average for comparable groups.

In Hartford, earned income averages about 65% of operating budgets. The Arts Council provides about 6% of the average budget; the remainder is obtained from individual contributions, private foundations, and government grants.

IV. **Why should business support the arts?**

A. First, it's good business.
1. Arts improve the quality of life. This makes it easier for companies to attract and keep good people.
2. The arts help bring tourists and conventions to Hartford.
3. Creativity is essential to business. Graphics and design are only the most obvious examples. The whole process of management is founded on creativity. A vital arts community provides the training and stimulus for creative people in all fields.
4. The arts comprise a $4 million local industry, employing hundreds of local people and providing substantial direct stimulus to the regional economy.

B. Second, the arts are important to society.
1. They enrich our individual lives, whether we take lessons or go to concerts or attend visual and performing events in our area.
2. Our children have good teachers—for piano, for drawing, for all the fine arts—because there are good artists in our area, drawn to Greater Hartford by the vitality of our cultural climate.
3. The arts help the underprivileged. They ameliorate the brutality of an impersonal existence for the elderly, for the poor, for the disadvantaged of all kinds.
4. One of our richest assets is our cultural heritage; we should not deny our children and future generations this same advantage.

V. **Why should contributions be made to the Arts Council instead of directly to the various arts?**

   A. The Arts Council is a united appeal. "One Gift for the Arts" means one solicitation, one contribution.

   B. The Council has four budget review committees, who carefully review arts organizations and their budgets. These volunteer committees, consisting of top level business executives and other concerned citizens ensure that these organizations are running lean and that contributions are going where they do the most good.

   C. The Arts Council provides in-kind services that help all arts groups operate more efficiently and effectively.

      1. Its Advocate Action Committee of business managers works directly with arts groups to improve their operations.

      2. The Council has specific programs to help arts groups increase their impact and revenues.

These answers give some of the basic information most frequently requested. Details on the Arts Council, its objectives and plans, the organizations it supports, and how it has disbursed its funds are provided in the accompanying annual report and white paper.

Schedule H-8

SOLICITOR REPORT FORM

Solicitor _____

Prospect	Goal	Pledge	Paid

Team _____

Vice Chairman_____

Data Verification	Comments
1. Right contact _____ 2. Employees _____ 3. Sales_____ 4. Other _____	
1. Right contact _____ 2. Employees _____ 3. Sales_____._____ 4. Other _____	
1. Right contact _____ 2. Employees _____ 3. Sales_____ 4. Other _____	
1. Right contact _____ 2. Employees _____ 3. Sales_____ 4. Other _____	
1. Right contact _____ 2. Employees _____ 3. Sales_____ 4. Other _____	

Exhibit I

INTRODUCTORY LETTERS

This exhibit contains a copy of the introductory letters sent out to all prospects of the Greater Hartford Arts Council three days before the kick-off of the 1977 fund drive. Schedule I-1 is the letter used for new prospects; Schedule I-2 is the letter used for past contributors.

NEW PROSPECT LETTER

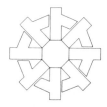

Greater Hartford Arts Council

W. Grant Brownrigg
Director

250 Constitution Plaza
Hartford, Connecticut 06103
(203) 525-8629

(Date)

(Name of Contact
Name of Corporation
Address)

Dear   :

67% of the executives interviewed in a recent national survey said that business has a responsibility to help support cultural activities in their community. They recognized that the arts are important in terms of providing

1. A high quality of life, which helps recruit good people.
2. A large number of skilled teachers.
3. A key attraction for tourists and conventions.
4. Direct economic benefits—jobs and local purchases— estimated at over $28 million per year in our state.

In Greater Hartford, we are fortunate in having local groups that are excellent in quality.... But they need your support.

As you can see by the enclosed brochure, the Arts Council is working to help the arts in our region. Within a few days, someone will be contacting you to ask for your help in our current fund drive. I hope you will join us in our effort.

I think an important point to consider is that any contribution you make will be matched on a 1 to 3 basis by the federal government, if the National Endowment's challenge grant is awarded to the Council. Thus, each dollar you give may produce $1.33 for the arts in Greater Hartford.

Sincerely,

WALTER J. CONNOLLY, JR.
President

Enclosure

OLD PROSPECT LETTER

Greater Hartford Arts Council

W. Grant Brownrigg
Director

250 Constitution Plaza
Hartford, Connecticut 06103
(203) 525-8629

(Date)

(Name of Contact
Name of Corporation
Address)

Dear   :

I am pleased to send you a copy of our Annual Report, which describes in detail our activities over the past year. I believe that you will find it useful and informative.

Our 1977 fund drive is about to begin. In a few days, someone will be contacting you to ask for your help in our campaign. I hope that you will be able to continue your generous support of the Arts Council.

Please note that any increase you make over last year's gift will be matched on a 1 to 3 basis by the federal government, if the National Endowment's challenge grant is awarded to the Council. Thus, each additional dollar you give may produce $1.33 for the arts in Greater Hartford.

Sincerely,

WALTER J. CONNOLLY, JR.
President

Enclosure

ABOUT ACA

The American Council for the Arts (ACA) is the leading private national organization that serves all the arts. Its services include advocacy for the arts, arts management training, news and publications. Its distinctive emphasis is on addressing needs that cut across art forms. ACA began its life eighteen years ago as a national association serving the newly forming state and community arts agencies. It has since broadened its membership to include performing arts organizations, museums, universities, libraries, arts centers, corporations, elected officials, professional arts managers and individual citizens, in addition to its historic constituency of arts councils and commissions.

ACA carries out its programs through monthly periodicals *(ACA Reports* and *Word from Washington)*, conferences, seminars, technical assistance, and specialized books for the field.

RELATED ACA PUBLICATIONS

A Guide to Corporate Giving in the Arts, Susan Wagner, editor.

> A detailed casebook which profiles individually the arts support programs of several hundred corporations. Each profile contains financial data, information about policy, factors affecting selections and levels of giving, areas of priority funding and who to contact with a proposal idea. Includes an introduction by Nancy Hanks and a chapter by Goldwin McLellan, President of the Business Committee for the Arts. $12.50

The Cultural Directory: Guide to Federal Funds and Services for Cultural Activities, Linda Coe, editor.

> Lists 250 programs of the Federal government that offer assistance to individuals and cultural organizations; cultural advisory groups; and relevant laws. Published with the Federal Council on the Arts and Humanities. $4.00

Finanacial Management for the Arts: A Guidebook for Arts Organizations, by Charles A. Nelson and Frederick J. Turk.

> Describes in clear, simple terms the non-artistic business aspects of the life of an arts organization. An indispensable guide. Published with assistance from the Shell Companies Foundation, Inc. $4.50

N
MA

A